To:_____

From:_____

Date:_____

sock monkey
Manners for Kids

Words and Pictures by Bethany Berndt Shackelford

HARVEST HOUSE PUBLISHERS
EUGENE, OREGON

Sock Monkey Manners for Kids

Text and artwork copyright © 2014 by Bethany Berndt Shackelford

Published by Harvest House Publishers
Eugene, Oregon 97402
www.harvesthousepublishers.com

ISBN 978-0-7369-5956-8

For more information about the artist, please contact
Suzanne Cruise Creative Services
PH: 913-648-2190

Design and production by BZB designer, Los Angeles, California
BZBdesigner.com

Printed in China

13 14 15 16 17 18 19 20 / LP / 10 9 8 7 6 5 4 3 2 1

For my two
little monkeys,
Tatum & Teaghan

Children, obey your parents in the Lord, for this is right.
"Honor your father and mother" (this is the first commandment with a promise),
"that it may go well with you and that you may live long in the land."
Ephesians 6:1-3

sock
monkey
Manners for Kids

Tip No. 1

Time to...

That means to make minor changes.

Do nothing from rivalry or conceit,
but in humility count others more significant than yourselves.
Philippians 2:3

sock
monkey
Manners for Kids

Tip No. 2

Try using...

manners

That can mean speaking politely
and using proper titles.

Even a child makes himself known by his acts,
by whether his conduct is pure and upright.
Proverbs 20:11

sock
monkey
Manners for Kids

Tip No. 3

Try serving...

munchies

Be a good host or hostess and offer your playmate a nutritious snack.

Show hospitality to one another without grumbling.
1 Peter 4:9

Secret Monkey Tip: For a sweet treat, try apple slices with cinnamon.

I'm miserable at jump rope.

I will never learn. I have two left feet.

sock monkey
Manners for Kids

Tip No. 4

Time to...

motivate

That means giving your friend
a reason to keep trying.

I can do all things through him who strengthens me.
Philippians 4:13

Thanks, Marius!

Hurray

You got it!
Jump, Melvin! Jump!
Jump, Melvin!
Jump!

I want to play ball.
I want to play with trucks.

I want to play ball.
I want to play with trucks.

I WANT to play BALL!
I WANT to play with TRUCKS!

sock monkey
Manners for Kids

Tip No. 5

Time to...

mediate

That means coming up with a compromise.

If possible, so far as it depends on you,
live peaceably with all.
Romans 12:18

Oh, no!
My truck is stuck.
Vroom
Vroom
ahhhhh!

Hurry, Milo!
There's a big boulder
rolling right toward you!
It's going to
crash...

sock monkey
Manners for Kids

Tip No. 6

Try to...

It means to mix together.

Let each of you look not only to his own interests,
but also to the interests of others.
Philippians 2:4

Whack!! Whack! WHACK!

Secret Monkey Tip: Leave lots of room for swinging the piñata stick.

Can you memorize the

6 Tips for **marvelous** Playdates

sock monkey Manners for Kids

Tip No. 1
modify
Make minor changes.

Tip No. 2
manners
Speak politely and use proper titles.

Tip No. 3
munchies
Offer your playmates a nutritious snack.

Molly   Mark   Max   Maddy   Mariu.

Tip No. 4
motivate
Give your friends a reason to keep trying.

Tip No. 6
mingle
Mix together.

Tip No. 5
mediate
Come up with a compromise.

* **Secret Monkey Tip:** Once you master the sock monkey manners, you will have lots of marvelous playdates!

Moe   Melvin   Milo   Maggie   Macy

Make Your Own
sock monkey

Traditionally sock monkeys are
made from "Rockford Red Heel Socks."
But you can get creative and use other kinds too.

Sock #1 will be used for the head, body, and legs.
Sock #2 will be used for the arms,
face, ears, and tail.

Sock No. 1

1 Turn both socks inside out.

2 Lay sock #1 down flat.
Draw a line in the center,
from the opening of the
sock at the bottom to about an
inch below the heel.

3 To make the legs,
sew across the bottom
and 1/4 inch away
from your line. Leave
about 1-inch opening
at the top so it can
be stuffed.

4 Cut along the
line to make the
monkey's legs.

5 Turn sock
right side out.

6 Stuff the whole thi
Sew opening closed.

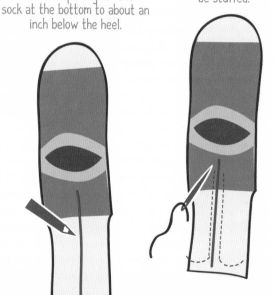

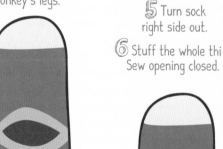

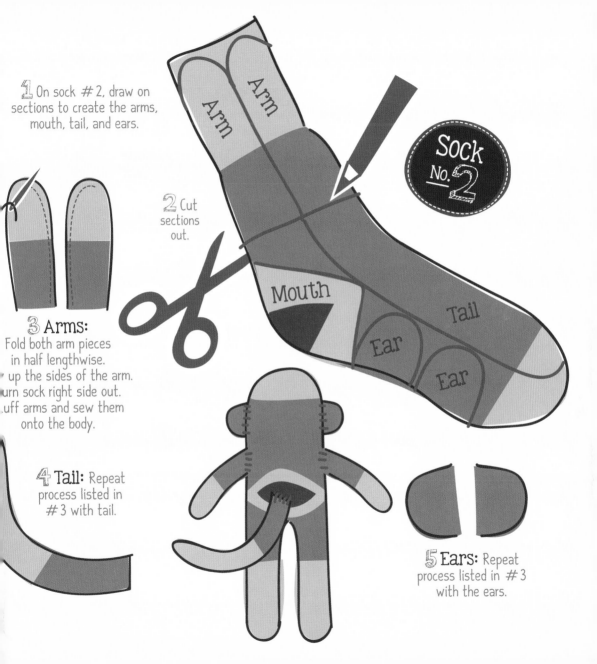

1 On sock #2, draw on sections to create the arms, mouth, tail, and ears.

2 Cut sections out.

3 Arms: Fold both arm pieces in half lengthwise. up the sides of the arm. urn sock right side out. uff arms and sew them onto the body.

4 Tail: Repeat process listed in #3 with tail.

5 Ears: Repeat process listed in #3 with the ears.

Arm

Arm

Mouth

Tail

Ear

Ear

Sock No. 2

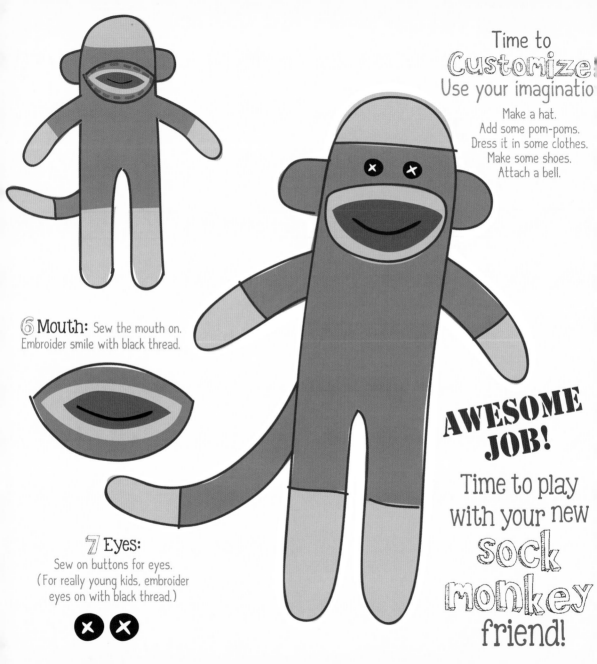

Time to **Customize!**
Use your imaginatio

Make a hat.
Add some pom-poms.
Dress it in some clothes.
Make some shoes.
Attach a bell.

6 Mouth: Sew the mouth on.
Embroider smile with black thread.

AWESOME JOB!

Time to play
with your new
sock
monkey
friend!

7 Eyes:
Sew on buttons for eyes.
(For really young kids, embroider
eyes on with black thread.)